# better together*

*This book is best read together, grownup and kid.

 akidsco.com

a
kids
book
about

# a kids book about therapy

by Sara Brenner, LCSW

# a
# kids
# book
# about

Printed in the United States of America.

A Kids Book About books are available online: *akidsco.com*

To share your stories, ask questions, or inquire about bulk
purchases (schools, libraries, and nonprofits), please use
the following email address: *hello@akidsco.com*

ISBN: 978-1-958825-03-7

Designed by Rick DeLucco
Edited by Jennifer Goldstein

For all the grownups doing
their best to build a brighter
future for the kids in their lives.

And to my mom and dad,
for giving that to me.

# Intro

I like to remind myself that more often than not, when kids go to therapy it's not their decision. They've been referred by a caring adult in their life (maybe a teacher, a doctor, a parent, etc.) for something they probably don't have any control over (grief, family changes, the way their brain works).

It's so important that we involve kids in every step of the process to empower them and make sure they feel heard, because that in itself is part of the healing process. Therapy can be a really abstract word—even for grownups—to try to define because it can look and feel so many different ways.

My hope for this book is to explain what therapy is, what to expect, and how it can be FUN! It can be a foundation for kids to build on for the rest of their lives.

Have you ever felt an emotion?

Have you ever experienced
a change in your life?

Have you ever wanted to understand yourself a little bit better?

Have you ever eaten a snack, had a nap, or taken a breath of air?

If you said yes to any of these...

# THEN THERAPY IS FOR YOU!

Hi, my name is Sara Brenner and I am a licensed clinical social worker.

Which is a really long way to say "therapist."

There are a lot of
different names for
the work I do like:

therapy,
counseling,
advocating,
helping,
teaching,
healing,
or comforting.

But for this book,
we'll just call it therapy.

You might be wondering...

WHAT EVEN

# IS THERAPY?

I'm glad you asked—that's what I'm here to talk to you about.

In therapy, you can learn about yourself, your thoughts, your feelings, and how you connect with the world around you.

In therapy, you can
work through challenges.

In therapy, you can be
honest about how you feel.

In therapy, you can be brave
in sharing your thoughts.

Some people who don't know
a lot about therapy might say...

It's only for broken people.

It's to try to fix you.

It's just talking to someone.

Or even that it's boring and no fun.

But therapy isn't any of those things.

Therapy is *not* something that exists to fix you.

Because guess what?!

# YOU'RE NOT BROKEN AND THERE IS NOTHING WRONG WITH YOU.

Therapy is for anyone who wants to live
a happy, healthy, more peaceful life.

Which means...

# THERAPY IS F

R EVERYONE!

And saying therapy is
"just talking to someone"
is like saying that when you
take your car to a mechanic
it's "just having someone
else look at it"!

No way!

It's going to a professional about something they're an expert about!

Since this might be the first time you're learning about therapy, maybe you're curious about what it's like.

So, let me explain a bit more...

# How do you
# get into therapy?

Well, because you're a kid,
a grownup would be the one
to find a therapist for you.

That means they would probably tell the therapist about you and why they thought therapy might be important for you.

Or you might be the one who says,
"I want to see a therapist."

And that's amazing!

# Where do you do therapy?

You'll probably meet in a small, private room with maybe a cozy chair, couch, or rug to sit on.*

*Or you might meet over video on a computer. Both are great options!

There might be cool art on the wall, books in a bookshelf, and even a few things to play with.

You may hear things like a sound machine, a fountain with splashing water, or some quiet music.

All of these things are there to help you feel safe and comfortable.

And a typical therapy appointment lasts for about an hour.

# What is
# a therapist?

A therapist is a
mental health* professional.

*Mental health basically means how we take care of our mind.

They go to school for
a really long time to train
to do this work.

But therapists also keep learning to know the best ways to support you.

Therapists are kind of like coaches,

but for your thoughts and feelings.

# NOW LET'S PAUSE.

Because there's something really important for you to know.

Your therapist is there for you.

**Yes, YOU!**

Not your grownup, not your teacher, not whoever brought you.

So, if you feel like you need
a new one, that's OK.

It's kinda like trying on clothes.

You want to find your style and the right fit, and most importantly, it needs to feel comfortable.

# What do you do in therapy?

You might talk about your opinions or your emotions.

You might play games or make something.

You might share about things that happened a long time ago, or yesterday, or today, or that you want to happen in the future.

You might pay attention to what you're feeling in your body.

Therapy should be fun and purposeful.

Because at the end of the day, your time in therapy is really about **you.**

What's really cool about therapy is...

No one makes you do something
you don't want to do.

You don't have to share
secrets you don't want to.

You won't get in trouble
for something you say.

Those things should never,
ever happen in therapy.

Make sure you tell
a grownup if they do.

And just so you know,
your therapist doesn't tell
anyone what you talk about.*

Not your teacher, grownup,
family, or your friends.

*Unless someone is in danger. Then it's very important to tell someone.

You might meet once
a week, or more, or less.

You might meet by yourself,
in a group, with your family,
or with your grownup.

# So, why should you go to therapy?

Because when you do...

You get to work through problems
you have in a supportive space.

You get to talk with a safe grownup
about things that feel scary.

You get to understand more about
why you think, feel, and act
the way you do.

You get to learn skills for how
to make your life feel less hard.

Therapy is a lot of things.

# IT'S FUN.
# IT'S BRAVE.
# IT'S CHALLENGING.
# IT'S EMOTIONAL.
# IT'S EMPOWERING.
# AND IT'S AWESOME!

Everyone has feelings, thoughts, and challenges.

Therapy helps you understand all of those things better.

Therapy isn't bad, scary, weird, or a waste of time.

# THERAPY IS HOW WE BECOME THE BEST VERSIONS OF OURSELVES.

# Outro

**Y**ou did it! Thank you for reading this book and looking for answers to some really important questions.

Right about now, you might be wondering "Now what?" And to that, my answer is: Keep the conversation going! Listen to what kids have to say after reading this book. Talk and ask about what they think therapy is, what they've heard about therapy before, how they feel about it, what they might like about it, and what worries they might have.

The possibilities for conversation are endless!

Being open and honest when you talk about therapy is a beautiful model for kids and will make it that much easier for them to share with a caring professional in that extra brave and supportive time with a therapist.

# About The Author

Sara Brenner (she/her), MSW, LCSW, PPSC, C-DBT, has earned a lot of letters behind her name (and is currently working towards adding even more) but her favorite title is what the kids she works with call her, "Miss Sara." Sara lives her life recklessly authentic and radically genuine. She is passionate about providing quality care to vulnerable and historically underserved populations, with the hopes of building a better future for each next generation.

Sara believes that every child deserves to feel safe, heard, empowered, valued, supported, and championed. Her hope is that this book can help make the idea of opening up and trusting someone new feel a little bit less scary and a lot more fun, because (as some 5th graders told her) therapy is cool.

@unfiltered.socialworker

a kids book about
BEING INCLUSIVE
by Ashton Mota & Rebekah Bruesehoff

a kids book about diversity

a kids book about LEADEr SHIP
by Orion Jean

a kids bo ak IMP
by MJ

a kids book about SAFETY
y Soraya Sutherlin, CEM
partnership with JUDY

a kids book about CLIMATE CHANGE
by Zanagee Artis Olivia Greenspan

a kids book about IMAGINATION
by LEVAR BURTON

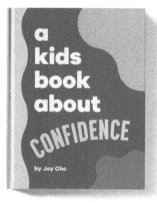

a kids book about CONFIDENCE
by Joy Cho

s ok out XIETY

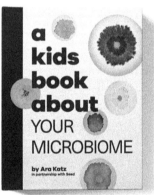

a kids book about YOUR MICROBIOME
by Ara Katz in partnership with Seed

a kids book about racism
by Jelani Memory

a kids book about DISABILITIES
by Kristine Napper

a ki b al b

a kids book about VORCE
Ashley Simpo

a kids book about cancer
by Dr. Kelsie Storm & Sarah Porter

a kids book about BEING TRANSGENDER
by Gia Parr
in partnership with The GenderCool Project

a kids book about DEPRESSION
by Kileah McIlvain

s ok out

a kids book about THE TULSA

Discover more at akidsco.com

Printed in the USA
CPSIA information can be obtained
at www.ICGtesting.com
LVHW071547021123
762909LV00011B/177